I0505372

THE SCIENTIFIC FORMAT:
ABSTRACT
INTRODUCTION
MATERIALS & METHODS
RESULTS
DISCUSSION
ACKNOLEDGMENTS
LITERATURE CITED
APPENDICES

www.ingramcontent.com/pod-product-compliance
Lightning Source LLC
Chambersburg PA
CBHW021438210526
45463CB00002B/563

* 9 7 9 8 6 2 0 7 4 1 2 5 0 *